OTHER HELEN EXLEY GIFTBOOKS
BY KATE TAYLOR
The Battle of the Sexes

Dedication: To all the men who made it possible...

Published simultaneously in 2003
by Exley Publications Ltd in Great Britain,
and Exley Publications LLC in the USA.

12 11 10 8 7 6 5 4 3

Selection and arrangement copyright
© Helen Exley 2003
Illustrations © Kate Taylor 2003
The moral right of the author has been asserted

ISBN 1-86187-592-4

Printed in China.

Exley Publications Ltd, 16 Chalk Hill, Watford, Herts WD19 4BG, UK.
Exley Publications LLC, 185 Main Street, Spencer, MA 01562, USA.
www.helenexleygiftbooks.com

OTHER HELEN EXLEY
GIFTBOOKS
Men! by Women
The Little Book of Stress
Too soon for a
Mid-Life Crisis
smile
Ms Murphy's Law
A Spread of Over 40s' Jokes

Looking for Mr Right

A HELEN EXLEY GIFTBOOK

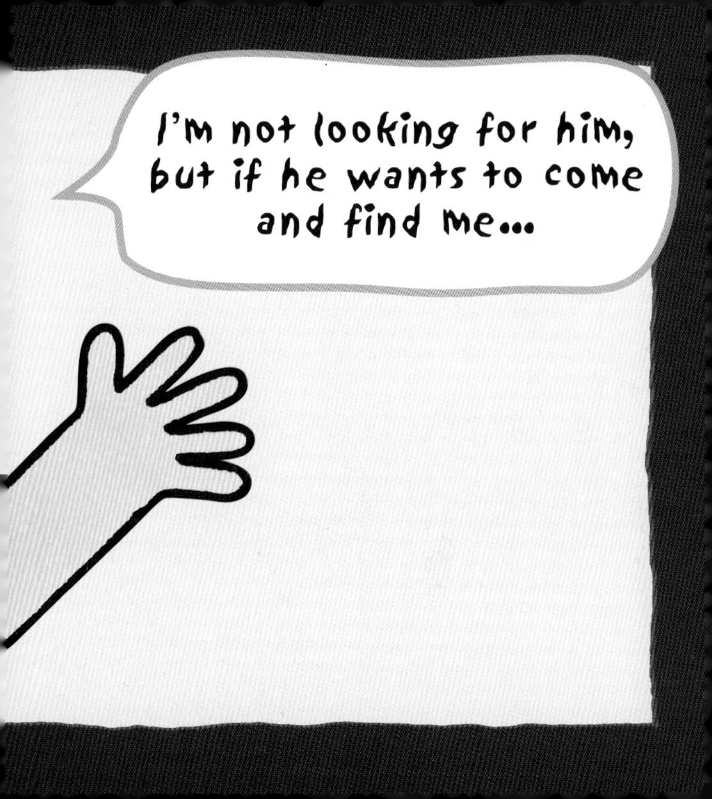
I'm not looking for him, but if he wants to come and find me...

It's our first date, but planning ahead, would you prefer a large or small wedding?

THE MAN-O-METER
Mr Right
Mr Almost Right
Mr Not Quite Right
Mr Wrong
Mr No Chance at all.

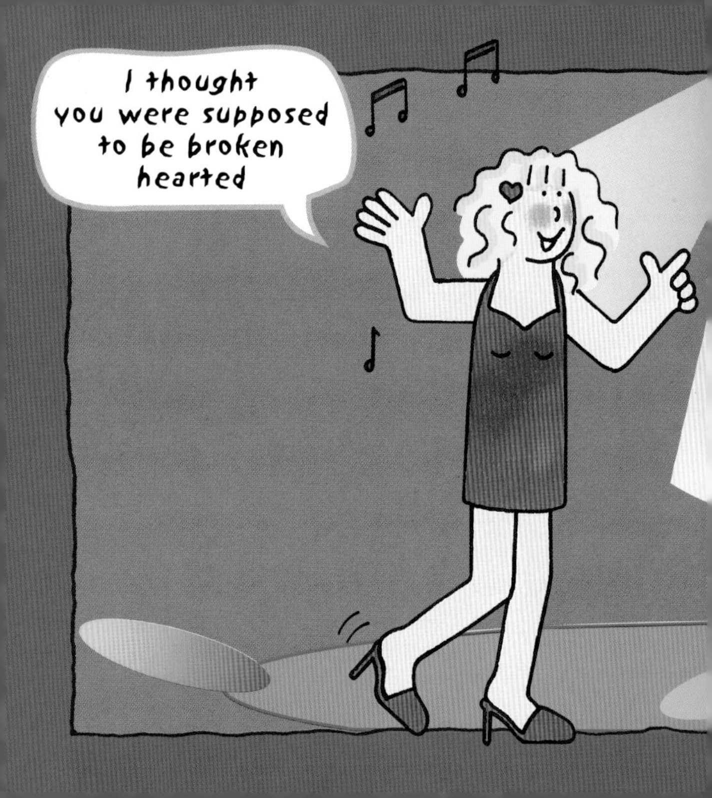
I thought you were supposed to be broken hearted

ABOUT KATE TAYLOR

Kate Taylor's 42, "but maybe you could put 30 (ish).... She went to art college from 1980-83 and since then has worked for an incredible number of magazines, design companies, greetings card companies, newspapers, advertising agencies and publishers, mainly in education and children's books. Her animated children's series, "Christopher Crocodile" for the BBC has sold around the world.

Kate Taylor feels she's an authority on looking for Mr. Right – and not finding him; "I am one step away from a tweed suit, comfy shoes and running a cat sanctuary."

"For me, I need the more athletic type of man, so I have recently taken up running. I ran my first marathon in London this year, and enjoyed it so much I went on to run Edinburgh and Helsinki and I have Berlin, Amsterdam and Honolulu planned before Christmas. I can't find Mr Right in the UK, so I'm going global..."

WHAT IS A HELEN EXLEY GIFTBOOK?

No expense is spared in making each Helen Exley
Giftbook as meaningful a gift as it is possible to create;
good to give, good to receive. You have the
result in your hands. If you have loved it –
tell others! There is no power on earth
like the word-of-mouth recommendation
of friends.

Helen Exley Giftbooks
16 Chalk Hill, Watford, Herts
WD19 4BG
185 Main Street, Spencer,
MA 01562, USA
www.helenexleygiftbooks.com

Also by Kate Taylor;
The Battle of the Sexes